I0766568

The Identification of

Hakka

Cultural Markers

By

Grace E. Wright

Copyright 2006
ISBN: 978-1-84728-592-8

____

Cover Image Pendant c1930 Hakka woman
Cover Photographs by Wesley Wright (2006)

TABLE OF CONTENTS

LIST OF FIGURES

Introduction

"The Hakka are the cream of the Chinese people." This statement, uttered by a Chinese missionary, identifies a group of people without making any specific references to actual cultural markers (Huntington 168). It presents a stereotypical view of a group of people who physically cannot be distinguished from Han Chinese. This is an investigation of the reality behind such a statement and defines the cultural markers distinguishing the Hakka from Han Chinese.

A review of the available materials in English reveals that the original discourse about the Hakka was written in the second half of the nineteenth century – a time when churches began establishing missions in

China. The missionaries who lived among the Hakka used a combination of sources; including personal observation, Hakka family genealogies and stories recounted to them, to write an assessment of the history and characteristics associated with the group of people known as the Hakka. In part these first attempts, due to unreliable sources and missionaries' motivations, presented stereotypical generalizations that either extolled the virtues of the Hakka, the people of their conversion efforts, or degraded the Hakka. However, these works did establish some reliable facts especially about the migration of the Hakka and provided the base for further studies on the Hakka in the twentieth century.

The second group of writings was published in the first half of the twentieth century when there were many attempts at writing comprehensive informational books about China. These compilations included the missionary accounts either verbatim or with minor alterations. For the purposes of this study these two groups: the missionary accounts and the early twentieth century compilations will be classified as Stage I in an effort to analyze what is the Hakka cultural identity. Stage II information is discourse written in the second half of the twentieth century, with a few exceptions. Most of the Stage II materials go beyond the original two groups and present further in-depth research or specialized investigation into various aspects of Hakka culture – though stereotypical characterizations still are present in some of these works.[1]

---

[1] Two bibliographies are at the end of this work: the first has the sources divided into Stage I and Stage II books; the second is the standard bibliography in alphabetical order.

Kashgar
Urumqi
Xinjiang
Lhasa
Inner Mongolia
Ningxia
Qinghai
Gansu
Tibet (Xizang)
Sichuan
Shaanxi
Xi'an
Henan
Shanxi
Hebei
Beijing
Tianjin
Liaoning
Jilin
Heilongjiang
Shandong
Jiangsu
Shanghai
Anhui
Hubei
Zhejiang
Hunan
Jiangxi
Guizhou
Fujian
Taiwan
Guangdong
Guangxi
Yunnan
Hainan

Origin

The Hakka, most scholars agree, are originally from north of the Yangtze River, even though most now live in the border areas of *Kwangtung (Guangdong)*, *Fukien (Fujian)* and *Kiangsi (Jiangxi)*. How and when they got to these areas has been a subject of mystery and debate since Westerners began studying the Hakka. Figure 1 categorizes some of the proposed migrational routes with the corresponding dates. The figure shows that all six authors that are charted agree that a Northern origin was likely. The provinces of *Shantung (Shandong)* (one author), *Shansi (Shanxi)* (two authors), *Anhwei (Anhui)* (three authors), *Honan (Human)* (two authors), *Kiangsi (Jiangxi)* (one author) and the Central Plains are all proposed as likely origin points of the Hakka migrations. Unless the Hakka were an amalgamation of several groups who moved at the same

FIGURE 1

Proposed Times of Hakka Migrations

Authors (see key below)		Date	Migration from	Migration to	1st MIGRATION	Possible Reason for Migration*
Stage I	Stage II	B.C.				
1 - 3 - 7		249-209	1 - 3 Shantung, Shansi, Anhwei	1 - 3 Honan, Anhwei, Kiangsi		Tsin Shi-Huan Persecutions
		A.D.				
1 - 5	2 - 4	317	4 Central Plains 5 Honan, Shansi & Anhwei	1 Jiangxi & Fukien 2 Central Kiangsi 4 Southern Hupei, Southern Hunan & Anhwei & Kiangsi 5 Southeastern Chekiang & Fukien & Southern Kiangsi		Disturbances between Tung-Chin and the Five Barbaric Races
3 - 7		419	7 Honan, Anhwei & Jiangxi	3 - 7 Southeastern Kiangsi (mountain regions) & borders of Fukien		Tsin Shi-Huan Persecutions
3 - 7		620		3 - 7 Fukien (mountain regions) & mountains between Jiangxi & Kwangtung		Tang persecution

5	4	880-11120	4 Anhwei, Honan, Kiangsi 5 Honan	4 Southern Anhwei, Southeastern Kiangsi, Southeastern Fukien, Northeastern Kwangtung 5 Fukien	2nd MIGRATION	Rebellion of Huang Chao
	2	907	2 Southern Fukien & Southwestern Fukien	4 Southern Anhwei, Southeastern Kiangsi, Southeastern Fukien, Northeastern Kwangtung 5 Fukien		
1		907-960		Southern Kiangsi-Fukien border		Barbarian invasions & ravages
1 - 7	2	1127-1280	2 - 7 Southern Fukien & Southwestern Fukien 7 Kiangsi	1 - 2 - 7 Kwangtung 7 Fukien	3rd MIGRATION	Barbarian invasions
5	4	1127-1644	5 Fukien 4 Southern Anhwei, Southeastern Kiangsi, Southeastern Fukien, Northeastern Kwangtung	4 - 5 Northern & Eastern Kwangtung		Yuan Invasion
1 - 3		1368	1 - 3 Kiangsi and Fukien	1 - 3 Kwangtung 3 Kwangsi		

Authors (see key below)		Date	Migration from	Migration to		Possible Reason for Migration*
1 - 7	2 - 4	1646	1 Kwangsi 2 Northern & Eastern Kwangtung 7 Fukien 4 Southern Anhwei, Southeastern Kiangsi, Southeastern Fukien, North & Eastern Kwangtung	1 Chungking region 2 - 4 Middle & Central Coastal areas of Kwangtung, Eastern & Central Szechuan, Eastern Kwangsi & Taiwan 7 West & Southwest of Canton	**4th MIGRATION**	Ch'ing encroachments
1 - 5		1723 - 1735	5 From mountain areas	1 - 5 West & Southwest of Canton		
1 - 3	2 - 4	1866 - and on		1 - 3 Kwangsi, Hainan, Formosa & overseas 2 - 4 Interior Kwangtung, Hainan Island, Overseas & Southwestern tip of mainland Kwangtung	**5th MIGRATION**	Punti-Hakka conflicts *most migrations also were prompted by famines resulting from invasions & natural causes

Key To Authors
For full citations see Bibliography

Stage I

1) Hsieh T'ing-Yu
3) Richards, L
5) Huntington, Ellsworth
   (used George Campbell as his source)
7) Ball, J. Dyer

Stage II

2) Cohen, Myron L.
4) Nakagawa, Manabu
   (used Lo Hsiang-lin as his source)

time to the South, no fixed point of origin can be agreed upon.[2]

Even with all of the discrepancies there is agreement that the Hakka probably made five waves of migration as reflected in Figure 1. The two migrations prior to 1127 may have been made by the progenitor groups of the Hakka. Therefore, it is only the last four waves, since 1127 that a group that can be identified as Hakka migrated. It is at this point that a form of agreement was reached by the six authors. At about the time of the Southern *Sung* Dynasty (1127 – 1279) all six authors agreed that the Hakka migrated from *Fukien* to *Kwangtung*. From this point forward the authors more or less agreed on the movements of the Hakka. Why? Prior to this time, information on the Hakka migrations came only from family genealogies and stories. These

---

[2] This, also, overlooks the likelihood of intermarriages by male migrants with local women in early generations and some intermarriage later in time.

records had possible inaccuracies and probably were based on partial myths. It was not until approximately Southern *Sung* time that written evidence of the Hakka group is available in government documents. (See map Figure 2 to locate areas of migration.)

The reasons for the migrations, however, are clear. Invasion from the north pushed people to move south. Chronic floods and droughts made migration for self subsistence sensible. Expeditions by neighboring groups to subjugate groups, including Hakka, encouraged them to move. Resettlement policies by the government also, encouraged the Hakka migrations (Richards 344, Nakagawa 214-215, Huntington 197-9, Cohen 243-251, Ball 281, & Hsieh 209-211).

There are a few theories about what genetic pool the Hakka originated from. George Campbell's view was that the Hakka were a "mongrel race more civilized than the aboriginals, but hardly entitled to rank with the

Figure 2 – Map of China

Chinese" (474). Others held the opposite view that the Hakka were "not foreigners but true Chinese" (Eitel 65). Many Hakka claimed a self-identification of Chineseness that was equal if not superior, to that of other Chinese (Leong 302). The *Punti* (native Han Chinese) claimed the Hakka were bandits, thieves and beyond the Chinese racial and cultural pale (Leong 306). Often times the Hakka reciprocated these feelings. They were known to refer to the *Punti* as a lazy, clever but malicious and a sneaking set of people who were descendants of aboriginal barbarians (Blake 2). The *Punti* despised the Hakka and often used the word "Hakka" as a derogatory designation to refer to a group of people, which Samuel Fearon in 1845 reported, "abandon without hesitation their hearths and household gods, their birthright and their father's tombs, to wander, unrespected, whither gain may call them." He continued the report by stating that the Hakka brought a demoralizing effect to the population that they settle amongst (Smith 108). These characterizations continued in 1905 when the Cantonese scholar Hunang Jie wrote <u>Guangdong Xiangtu Lishi</u> (a school history of *Guangdong*) that the Hakka were referred to as "not of Han racial stock" (Leong 308).

Other more recent theories bring new ideas and technologies to bear on the mystery. Enthnographically Lo Hsiang-lin proposed Hakka could be considered an "ethno-stemmata" – a segment of the Chinese population that is pure Chinese with "its own language, customs, and conventional ways of living, showing marked differences to other various ethno-stemma" (Nakagawa 215-6). Another view is that of Clyde Kiang who uses the genetic work of Dr. Matsumoto Hideo that classifies the Hakka with the Japanese, Koreans and Mongolians. He does not view the Hakka as Chinese racially (Kiang 7).

The name, Hakka, most scholars believe was fixed sometime between the *Sung* (960-1279) and *Yuan* dynasties (1279-1368) not as a racial classification but rather to designate a group of displaced Chinese people (Han 23, Nakagawa 216).[3] Hakka (*Kejia or K'ohkias*) has been translated in various ways with "guest people," "strangers," "squatters" or "aliens" as the most common. The name was descriptive of a group of people who, because of migrations, were not the original inhabitants of the regions that they occupied (Hsieh 218). It was applied in order to distinguish the Hakka from the more established inhabitants or "native inhabitants" (*Punti*) in local registers. The term was used in a manner that E. J. Eitel in 1867 referred to as "politely humiliating" (265). Leong differed from this view and endorsed the idea that "Hakka" had commonly been mistaken as a label given

---

[3] Ting-Yu Hsieh places the date earlier. He said the term originated circa A.D. 780 when it appeared in the T'ang census (217).

by others, when in fact it was a term of self-designation (291). While Hsieh contends the name was given to the group and that the Hakka "renounced the name as degrading to their dignity" (202). Blake explained the discrepancy with the view that how the word "Hakka" was intoned or modified conveyed either contempt or respect (49).

Language

In 1993 the fifth largest linguistic group in mainland China, with approximately 20 million speakers, with a dialect that was one of the most identifiable cultural markers was the Hakka people (Yun 9). Study of the Hakka dialect by Westerners began when missionaries analyzed different Chinese dialects in order to proselytize in local dialects and translate religious materials for distribution. Missionaries' research compiled the following data (Chart 1) on the Mandarin, Hakka and Cantonese (*Punti* or *Bendi*) dialects:

Chart 1 -- Dialects

DIALECT:	Mandarin	Hakka	Cantonese
Number of sounds (syllables):	532	619	700 to 707
Number of tones:	4 or 5	6	8
Pronunciation:		7 of 10 words are phonetically transition words	

Taken from: E. J. Eitel – 1887 (267),
R. Lechler – 1878 (356),
L. Richards – 1908 (207) and
Dyer Ball – 1925 (183).

From the collected data and the perceived pronunciation of Hakka it seemed evident to Stage I authors that the Hakka dialect was not only an independent branch of the common Chinese language but that it was a connecting link between the Mandarin and Cantonese dialects (Eitel 267). The question was: What was the connection between the three dialects and could a determination be made about which was the original dialect? As shown in Chart 2, Stage I authors, though divided on which dialect was the original, were

unified in their belief that Hakka stood as the connecting

language between Mandarin and Cantonese.

Chart 2 – Connected Languages Stage I

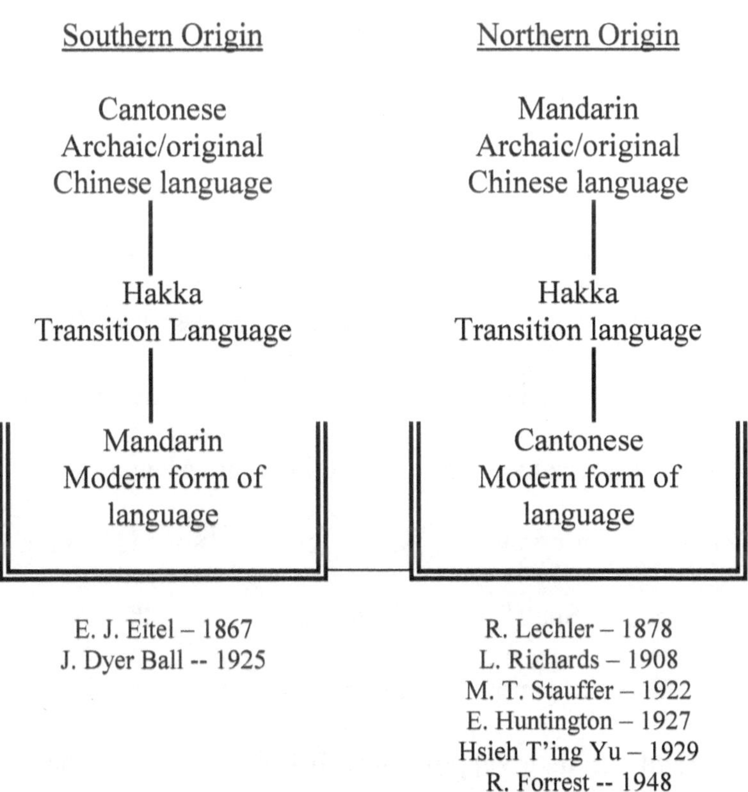

Two Major theories about origin and classification of
the Hakka language by Stage I authors.

As Chart 2 indicates some determined that Hakka was a "crystallized relic" of one phase through which the Chinese language had passed in developing from Cantonese to Mandarin (Eitel 265). Others determined that the transition had gone the other way with the Mandarin dialect as the original stock of the Hakka and Cantonese dialects. As R. Lechler wrote in 1878 "from Mandarin other dialects branched off in the course of time" and Hakka was one (Lechler 1878). Hakka they deduced stood between Northern Chinese (Mandarin) and Cantonese but closet to the former. They further stated that Hakka was less polite than Mandarin but more "conservative" with "clearer sounds" than Cantonese (Stauffer 351, Forrest 237). The adherents of the different camps used the numbers shown in Chart 1 to reinforce their suppositions. If Hakka had a Northern origin the numbers indicated that the language improved with an expansion to more syllables and tones. This trend then continued in the transition from Hakka to Cantonese (Lechler 356). If the origin came from the South the changes in numbers indicated a refinement of the language to fewer syllables and tones. Either way, per Stage I authors, Hakka occupied a middle position between an archaic and modern form of the Chinese language.

In 1937 Li Fangkuei proposed the division of modern Chinese dialects into seven major groups (Norman 181, Ramsey 87). Chart 3 shows the classifications. (Linguistic Maps Figure 3 and 4)

Chart 3 – Connected Languages Stage II

Major theories about the
origin and classification of
the Hakka language for
Stage II authors

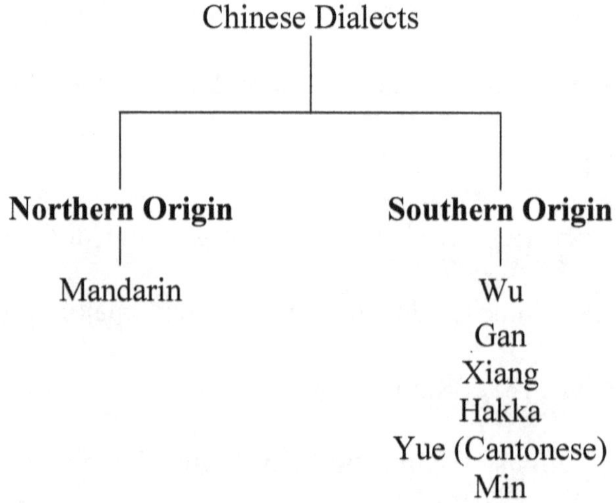

Origins of the Seven Chinese Dialects

S. Robert Ramsey – 1987
Jerry Norman – 1988

Figure 3 – Lingustic Map (Kwangtung)

THE PROVINCE OF KWANGTUNG -- LANGUAGE AREAS

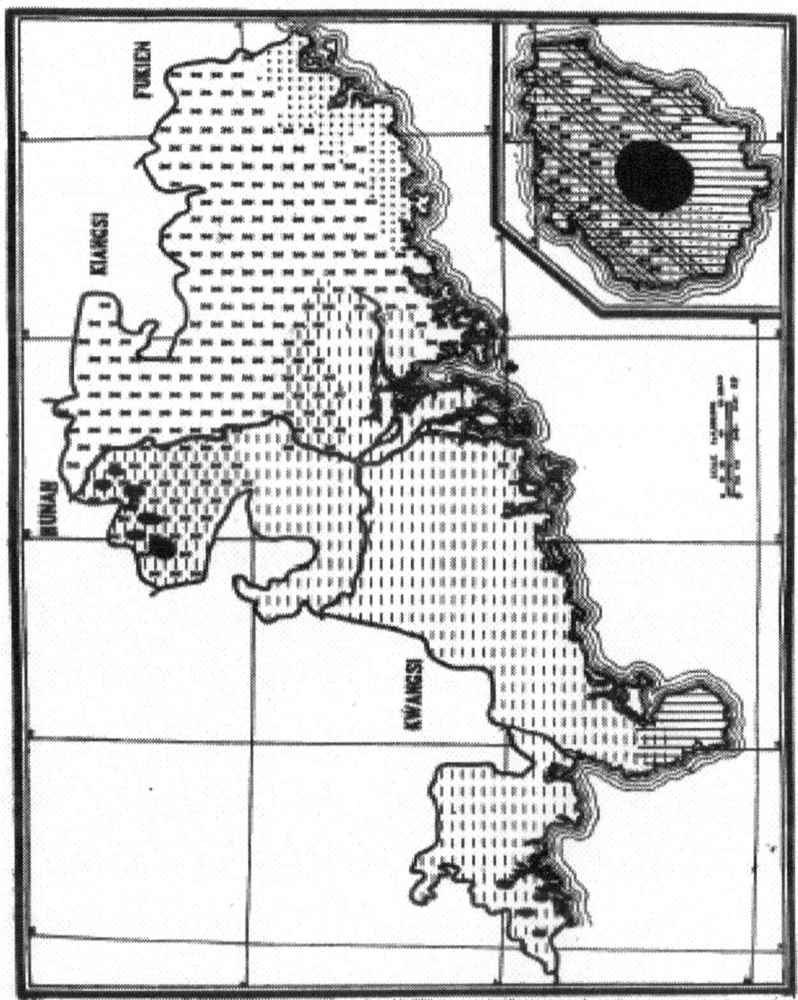

Milton T. Stauffer 1922

NOTE: Horizontal lines indicate Cantonese-speaking areas and vertical lines Hainanese-speaking districts. The small shaded areas are inhabited by aboriginal tribes, whose languages are unknown and among whom no missionary work is done. The small crosses indicate the Hakka-speaking areas. Throughout the dotted area in southeast Kwangtung the Hoklo language is spoken. The diagonal lines in Hainan as well as the small dots indicate the presence of Miao and Tai tribes each speaking distinct languages.

Figure 4 – Lingustic Map

S. Robert Ramsey 1987

As shown in Chart 3 Hakka has been classified as a division of the Chinese language from the Southern developmental branch – it does not link Mandarin and Cantonese. It is a separate dialect that is no more closely related to Mandarin than Cantonese (Norman 227). Even though the Hakka people have historical geographic origins that seem to lay in the North linguistically the base of the Hakka dialect developed almost surely in Northeastern Guangdong from a variety of Chinese dialects present in South China since the Han dynasty. Hakka does have some unmistakable Northern features but the vocabulary is characteristically Southern and the syntactic structure is generally of the Southern type (Norman 112, Ramsey 111). Hakka is clearly not a transition language between Mandarin and Cantonese.

There have been some other theories on the classification of the Hakka dialect as S. Robert Ramsey stated "once some linguists grouped Gan and Hakka together as Gan-Hakka" because both showed a development of aspirated consonants. Ramsey however, says that, currently, linguists can find no other reason for the grouping and therefore have generally abandoned it as a possibility (111). Another theory placed the Central Plains as the place of origination of the Hakka dialect (Moser 78). Kiang also endorsed this theory in 1991 when he wrote "*Han Hua*, the official language of Han people in the central plains, may be the true spoken language of the Hakka people and *Han Hua* was evolved into Hakka (53)."[4] This theory, also has been abandoned as modern linguists through research on syntactic structure, vocabulary and pronunciation have

------

[4] I have reservations about the scholarship that is presented in Clyde Kiang's work. It should be read carefully before accepting the information presented.

firmly placed the Hakka dialect as one of Southern origination.

Language was a means of group affiliation and had been an easy way to distinguish Hakka from other cultural groups. Marshall Broomhall summarized the Hakka as a group that "clan together, speaking their own language and preserving their own customs" (Broomhall 64, Cohen 241). Burton Pasternak stated that "We find little to suggest Hakka were inherently different from other Southeastern Chinese in the matter of social organization" -- so what besides language distinguished the Hakka from other cultural groups?

Livelihood

At the beginning of the 20th century the economic base of a Hakka village was agriculture.[5] The Hakka were repeatedly referred to as "excellent cultivators of the soil" and "they are a frugal, thrifty, persevering race, and as farmers and laborers excel the Puntis" (Broomhall 44). The Hakka primarily cultivated rice; potatoes, after the Portuguese introduced them around 1500, and vegetables (Blake 10). B. C. Henry in his travels in South China noted that "Wherever they [Hakka] settle they plant fruit and other trees and the place begins at once to assume a thrifty, prosperous look" (273). The Hakka became known as uncommonly able people. Ellsworth Huntington surmised that because of migration the Hakka suffered natural selection where the weaker or more conservative

---

[5] This is consistent with the livelihood of most of China at the time.

elements were left behind. So it was the most able and energetic who settled in the new home (167, 194). Hakka, however, did not work just in the fields. Hakka men were known to leave their homes and hire themselves out for labor or war. In this way many men found their way to cities like Canton, Singapore, Siam, Formosa and the Dutch East Indies (Huntington 167, Han 27).

J. Dyer Ball and F. J. Wiens characterized Hakkas in the city as "wide-awake and intelligent in character"[6] and found in most of the responsible places and occupations of South China. Hakka men were employed on railroads, boats, as coolies, barbers, stonecutters, foreign ladies' tailors and in telegraph offices. Campbell noted that "The railroad between *Chao-chaufu* and Swatow was built by Hakka

---

[6] This probably refers to men hired as laborers in the city not to women.

contractors and is now owned and largely manned by Hakkas" (474). According to Ellsworth Huntington, if you asked a coolie or merchant in Canton about the Hakka coolies their reply was "Hakka are a barbarous degraded set of people, little better than bandits, who take no care of their women, and who are a danger to every one else." Huntington felt this response was because the native coolies feared the more competent Hakka coolie would supplant the less competent Cantonese worker. This was consistent with the characterization that Hakka men were ambitious, manly and vigorous race (Broomhall 44).

As well, Hakka were found in educational institutions.[7] (F. J. Wiens 6-7, Ball 281, Richards 207). Their value of education was another well known stereotype – a value that they shared with the dominate Han culture. Education was typified as a means to

---

[7] It is not clear if they were students, teachers or both.

compensate for the relatively low remuneration from trade and agriculture in their highland districts and Hakka were famed for their determination to seek an education despite poverty and hardship (Yun 10). Marshall Broomhall in his description of the Hakka said they were "better educated than those in the more crowded plains" (44). Harry J. Lamley stated that during the *Qing* period "many Hakka men sought to advance themselves by earning academic degrees" (288). During this period Hakkas were able to acquire gentry status by means of the prefectural examinations, which was a standard practice in Chinese society. In prefectures, where Hakka formed a substantial minority, special quotas for military and civil examinations were established for them to ensure Hakka individuals had an avenue to government jobs. This was a practice the Manchus had instituted for most minority groups to integrate them into the mainstream of Han society

32

(Leong 295). As most stereotypes the characterization was not applied uniformly to all Hakka as stated by F. J. Wiens – there are "some [Hakka] highly educated and really refined" and "some [Hakka who practice the] worst kind of brutality and cannibalism" (7). All of these characteristics, also, were applied to other cultural groups and were mere generalizations used to keep groups segregated and relegated to a lower status. Therefore, they cannot be used to define the cultural identity of the Hakka. Perhaps the most defining feature was that Hakka men left home to acquire additional resources to supplement agricultural income. This feature left Hakka women at home to care for the family fields.

Female Markers

Women in Hakka society have always been defined by three dominant characteristics: 1) large feet 2) hardworking and 3) distinctive apparel. These three characterizations are found in almost all of the Stage I material. The first characteristic was an accurate cultural marker and is explained by the fact that Hakka women never practiced foot-binding. Foot-binding may have started in court circles, spread to the upper classes and then to the peasant class. The practice began in the Southern *Sung* dynasty (1127-1278) and it probably reached its peak during the Ming dynasty (1368-1644). The Manchu rulers of the succeeding *Qing* (*Ch'ing*) dynasty (1644-1911) never followed the practice – in fact they banned it several times. The practice died out

in the early twentieth century.[8] It should also be noted
that many Chinese peasant women left their feet
unbound for economic reasons. So, unbound feet were
not exclusive to Hakka women but as R. Lechler notes:
"high and low of the [Hakka] female sex preserve their
natural feet, which gives them a very different standing
in society" (358).

Other physical attributes attributed to Hakka
women in Stage I writings were rather subjective. Han
Suyin states that Hakka women, even if they lived in the
city, did not "bind their breasts" (27).[9] This practiced
predominately by city women began later than foot-
binding and lasted into the early twentieth century.

---

[8] The Manchu issued repeated edicts banning the practice, the last
of them in 1902, but with little effect. The Republic of China
banned foot-binding in 1912 and the practice was again banned by
the People' Republic of China in 1949, but it is likely the practice
had already been abandoned at this time. Levy, Howard S. Chinese
Footbinding. New York: Bell Publishing Co., 1967.
[9] There were no other references to this particular practice so it
could not be verified if the majority of Hakka women did not bind
their breasts. It seems likely that Hakka women who worked in the
fields and who Han also says did not hire wet nurses did not bind
their breasts.

Ellsworth Huntington in his 1927 work The Character of Races stated that Hakka "women are unusually pretty" (168) and George Campbell said they are "strong and erect" but a bit "undersized" because of the excessive toil begun early in life (473). While Han Suyin in 1965 wrote the opposing view that Hakka women are tall and big-boned "not renowned for good looks" (27). It is clear that Hakka women, like any other culture, had some women who met differing criteria of physical attributes. Many of the particular attributes noted in the Stage I works were advantageous to and therefore related to the labor that Hakka women performed.

The characterization of being hard working was not as concrete as large feet. From the earliest English writings on the Hakka (Stage I) it was noted that Hakka culture, unlike other Chinese cultures, had a difference in the definition of the division of labor by gender. Hakka women worked in the fields and carried burdens

(Campbell 473, Alley 1973, 21) as R. Lechler said "You meet them [Hakka women] carrying heavy loads which you would rather wish to see put on men's shoulders, and they seem never to have had enough leisure to learn proper woman's work, so that they are generally obliged to engage a tailor to make their dresses" (359).[10]

It is certain that Hakka women not only managed the household but also worked along with the men in the fields to produce grain (rice). They also worked the fields alone even using "water buffalo with equanimity" when their "menfolk went off to fight" or went in search of jobs (Alley 1973, 21, Kazuko 1). Conditions of their daily existence often made it necessary for Hakka women to be self-reliant. Often they were responsible for the entire cycle of agricultural tasks from plowing to harvesting. This necessitated self reliance, which may

---

[10] Later in his article Lechler does state that "[Hakka] women spin cotton, and are also able to weave the yarn into cloth, of which they make their winter dresses."

even have included defense of their homes (Han 27, Blake 51).

This labor naturally made them stronger physically in comparison to Han women. This fact produced an image of innate physical strength that would follow them as they moved to new homes. Blake wrote that after 1960, in the New Territories, the labor of digging and carrying mud, sand and gravel was predominately done by Hakka women. In fact, employers, because of the stereotype, preferred to hire Hakka women for these jobs. The records of a medical missionary who worked among the Hakka indicated the most frequent complaint of Hakka women was chronic backache (Blake 55). So the image was based on increased physical abilities from work not on an innate quality. A history of female labor in the fields was a clear difference compared to other Chinese cultures.

This can be identified as a cultural marker for the Hakka.

Female Attire

Reference to distinctive Hakka female clothing included only a few items in the Stage I works. The most commented on piece of apparel was a broad brimmed hat, the *liangmao* (cool hat), which was approximately 40 centimeters in diameter, with a valance of cloth around it that was approximately 10 centimeters wide.

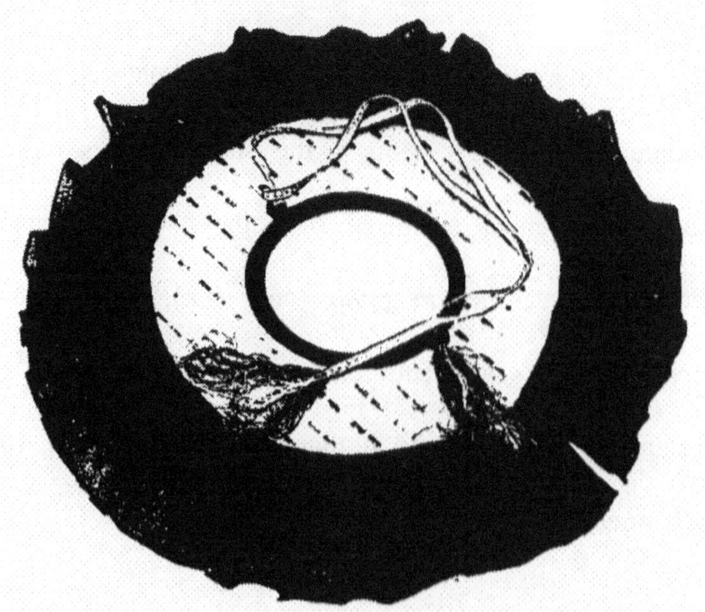

The hair done in a top-knot went through the opening at

the crown of the hat (Ball 280, Blake 109). While

working in the fields the hat was very practical as a sun

shade and could be used as a means to carry small items

such as combs and knives slipped under the tie. If the

hat was not worn, an embroidered head-band was bound

around the head (Alley 1973, 21). J. Dyer Ball states

that the band looked "something like an old fashioned bonnet" (198). In the ears Hakka women wore trumpet shaped silver ornaments with rings of silver closely spaced along the edge or they commonly wore earrings that were a silk tassel (Ball 199, 280). J. Dyer Ball also comments that Hakka jackets differed from Cantonese jackets in that the "jacket was longer reaching nearly to the knees" and that the Hakka shoes had "square toes," which makes sense for women who had unbound feet (280). Another item associated with Hakka women was a long sash of apron fabric tied around the waist (Piton 219).

This sash may have been what Elizabeth Johnson calls the *fa tai* or patterned band.[11] (Figures 6 & 7) The band was worn by Hakka women as an article of personal adornment.

---

[11] Elizabeth L. Johnson's work was done in the New Territories of Hong Kong. As well several of the other Stage II works were done in Taiwan or the New Territories of Hong Kong not in mainland China.

Patterned bands are hand woven, intricately patterned ribbons about 1 CM wide, and ranging in length from about 65-145 CM. They are most commonly flat, with tassels of varying length and thickness at either end, and are either multicoloured, or white with coloured or black patterns. If multicoloured, they are made of silk (now often synthetic) threads with silk tassels; if white, they are of cotton with the patterns in silk or cotton and the tassels of white cotton cord (1976, 81). (Figures 6 and 7)

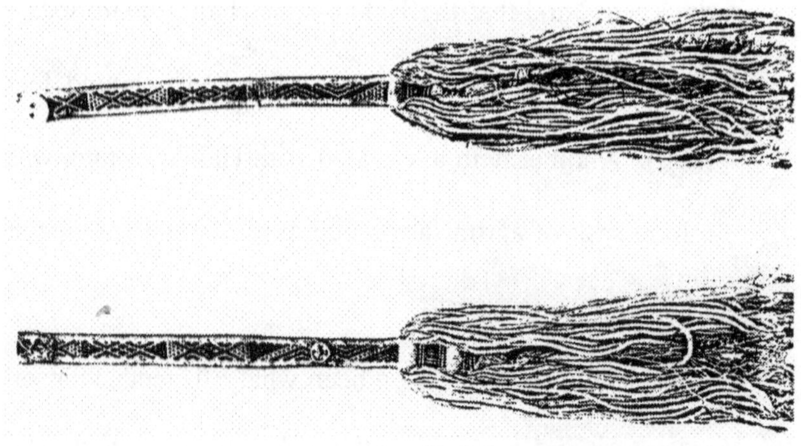

Figure 6 -- Patterned Bands with Tassels

Figure 7 -- Patterned Bands

Another type of band was tubular rather than flat and was worn only as an apron band in the summer. Patterned bands were the only ornamental apparel worn by tradition-all-dressed Hakka women in the New Territories, with the exception of some simple jewelry. The band can be worn in several ways. It often was worn as an ornament on the characteristic hat commonly worn by Hakka women while working in the sun. It was either cut in half then sewn on either side of the hat's center hole or the band was used to tie the hat under the

wearer's chin.  An uncut band also may have been used to hold the rectangular head cloth worn by Hakka women both indoors and outdoors when a hat was not worn. The band was passed over the head cloth and fastened on the back of the head below the hair bun leaving the tassels hanging as an ornament. A third use was to fasten a small apron across the back. To accomplish this small buttons were sewn to the band and then put around the neck and buttoned to the apron (Johnson 81-3). These descriptions bare a striking resemblance to what was written by the Stage I authors about Hakka female apparel.

According to Johnson, the bands also served other purposes at important events in life. At the time of marriage a bride gave them as "gifts to all the older women relatives who came to attend the festivities." They were used to tie back the mosquito nets on the marriage beds and tied around the foot-washing basin that was an important dowry item and fertility symbol. When a son was born, a "long red patterned band was hung over the lantern" in the ancestral hall at the *hoi tang* ceremony to symbolize the birth (1976, 81-3).

Elizabeth Johnson also confirmed what R. Lechler said in 1878 that Hakka women "did little, if any, embroidery, home weaving of fabrics, or sewing; this work was generally done by specialists." The main reasons were poverty and the fact that all Hakka women not only did the household chores and childrearing but the younger women did most, if not all, of the agricultural work and did heavy carrying work for wages. Women as noted in Stage I works often managed the fields when Hakka men were away working so little time was left to weave (1976, 84). They however, wove bands in the evenings, on bad weather days, agricultural slack seasons and at festivals. Weaving the patterned bands was complex and difficult to learn. The technique was taught by older female relatives to a girl when she was in her teens (Johnson 1976, 85).

The band's colors and designs expressed aspects of the wearer's identity. The colors and color combinations were used to indicate marital status and the regional affiliation of the wearer. As well, the length and thickness of the tassels indicated regional affiliation. A woman, upon marriage and moving to a new region, continued to wear the patterned bands of her own native area therefore, always identifying her place of origin (Johnson 1976, 87-9). It has been noted by Stage II writers that the traditional Hakka hat is worn by other groups and the patterned band also may be used by other cultural groups. Therefore, neither can accurately be identified as a cultural marker in present society.

Singing and Stories

Wolfram Eberhard said that the Hakka were "famous everywhere for their love of singing" and that they were "the most song-loving ethnic group among the Han Chinese" (56, 104). Their love songs (called *qingge*) are said to date back to the Han dynasty and are sung by women or at times both male and female sing in response to each other (Han 25, Eberhard 57). These mountain songs were melodic, ballad-like songs with themes of love (Kazuko 3; Johnson 1988, 137). (Example 1) On occasion, a single song could last for nearly half an hour – "the leisurely verses and extended codas fading only to return full force as if there would be no end" (Kazuko 2). Other types of songs included impromptu flirting songs, musical battles between a man and a woman, laments by brides before their weddings, and laments by women during funerals.

Borrowing an Undershirt

Man:
  The north wind is blowing and I'm in a panic
  I want to borrow some winter clothing from you.
  I don't want your short jacket or long padded gown.
  What I want most of all is your undershirt.

Woman:
  An undershirt is an undershirt.
  If I loan it to you, then I'll be cold.
  But I'll leave the buttons on my gown undone,
  And the collar on my jacket unfastened.
                                    (Kazuko 3)

Elizabeth Johnson's study of Hakka death laments brings a new aspect to the role of songs in Hakka culture as it relates to women. Her study gives a window into a Hakka woman's grievances and values. (Example 2) The laments called "weeping" or "weeping for a broken fate" deal with personal relations and show a belief in equality and fair treatment in the family. The laments are sung by women alone at the wake of an older relative. In the lament the singer may mourn the effect of the death on her life in addition she may criticize relatives for past slights or injustices. "Virtually all the laments state her need for recognition and fair treatment, whether from living relatives, the deceased, or the hand of fate" (Johnson 1988, 138). Though the themes of equality and fair treatment are not strong in the dominant ideology, they do not threaten male-dominated structures of household and lineage. Therefore, the songs were uninterrupted by the males of the household.

Example 2:

Death Lament

(A lament of a woman married into a poor household
upon the death of her mother)

My mother listened to others
And married out this dead-fate, struggling girl.
I am so poor that I carry loads
Until my shoulders look like rough granite.
If I had been married better
I would not be so wretched now.
My feet are full of holes
Like a rice-drying basket.

Singing laments at funerals is not exclusive to Hakka culture. The same practice can be found in many other cultures. What the Hakka laments do is give valuable information about Hakka women's lives, which cannot be obtained through other historical sources. Death laments themselves, sung by Hakka women, can not be used to define the Hakka cultural identity.

Similar to folk songs is Wolfram Eberhard's collection of Hakka folktales. He found that few tales were exclusively Hakka and not found in other ethnic groups in China (145). He also was unable to determine the origin dates of the tales. This makes the tales an unreliable source for Hakka history but does provide some insight into more recent Hakka culture. Folktales can be a means to reaffirm a group's identity and convey positive social values. Also, the ways in which Hakka tellings of the tales shift emphasis or add or delete elements from the tales is significant when compared to Han or other versions.

Eberhard found that besides the traditional Confucian values there were some virtues extolled that were not typically Confucian. These included 1) the reward of good deed and honesty 2) greed as bad and wealth at the base of unhappiness 3) hard work led to wealth 4) mean actions were punished 5) criminals were always found out and 6) fighting brought profit only to a third person. Belief in fate, which was also not Confucian, Eberhard found in one tale (97-8). He also found that there were no creation myths for the beginning of the world and for objects in the world. As well, the netherworld was not mentioned nor was rebirth or Buddhist deities (142-3). The following (Example 3) is a folktale that Eberhard relates that can be analyzed in parts to show what cultural myths and characteristics are expressed to show a positive Hakka culture. Many of the characterizations are the stereotypes that can be found in Stage I works.

Why Can Hakka Girls Sing Mountain Songs?

Folktale: Formerly there was a Hakka who was governor of Guangdong (Kuang-tung) province. He had money and power, and at that time he would get whatever he wanted to get. In spite of that he never married three wives or four concubines, but lived very well with his old wife.

Analysis: A Hakka can hold a high position in government, which typically is gained only through education. Even with a high position Hakka men are not greedy and remain faithful in a monogamous marriage. The Hakka were moral people.

Folktale: I have heard that came about because in his youth he had been very poor, and because his wife had suffered the poverty together with him, had earned money so that he could study. When he later became a high official, he never forgot the good heart of his wife or his former years.

Analysis: He started poor like most Hakka but by working together in a system of "mutual support" with his wife he was frugal and wisely used his money not for immediate gain but for future rewards through education. When he received his reward he equally shared it with his hard working wife.

56

Folktale: This tells us about the origin of the equality of
love of the Hakka women, but it also tells us
how the equality of sexes among Hakka girls and
boys had its origin, and that it is not a hollow
word, but that the women with both feet on the
ground carry on the problems of the family
together with the men.

Analysis: Women in a Hakka household are equal
because they participate in all of the daily
activities both inside and outside of a household.
Of course they are able to do this because they
do not have bound feet.

Folktale: And because Hakka women can live without
men, they are not afraid if the men cheat upon
them – they just cannot cheat on them. Hakka
girls have the courage to take their fate into their
own hands and sing it openly out in their
"Mountain Songs"

Analysis: Women are equal and can manage without a
man. The man knows he is not needed therefore
he remains faithful to his wife. Women feel a
freedom with this equality and therefore can
practice self determination.

Folktale: The Hakka are people who had to flee from
suppression, and their surroundings are all poor,
and so they all have to endure together. If one
has to suffer, the others will help him, and so the
Hakka girls work just as their men do; in contrast
to other women, the Hakka women have as the
first ones gained their position, and so they also
sing songs which the others do not sing (104-5).

Analysis: The Hakka individually and as a group have
suffered.   Hakka history has been one of

migration. It is the group solidarity that has seen them through the hard times. The suffering has helped women to gain equality and escape the repression that other cultural groups place on their women. Therefore, Hakka women are more daring and open.

Hakka Characterizations Extolled in the Tales:

value education	monogamous unions
hardworking	honor the wife
history of migration	female equality
group solidarity	unbound feet
mutual support	gender equality in work

Marriage & Family

Folktales are typically used to bind a group together and to instill and reinforce behaviors. They are often told within a group activity and children grow up hearing these tales but in Stage I works very little is said about the role of children in Hakka culture. J. Dyer Ball mentioned that female infanticide was prevalent among the Hakka while Han Suyin, in agreement, stated that in the past the Hakka did not tolerate crippled or defective babies. These children were left to die immediately after birth (Ball 300, Han 26). It also was mentioned in the Stage I works that a family would rather kill a daughter then sell her into concubinage. Han stated that Hakka women did not hire wet nurses but tended to the babies themselves (27). The only other mention about children revealed that children wore a ring of silver around their neck (Ball 280). In Stage II Elizabeth

Johnson relayed a conversation with an 80 year old woman that gives some insight into childhood for a Hakka. The women told of her life.

> . . . when I was eight or ten years old I began to cut grass and carry firewood. I went with a group of girls, never alone. I was married when I was sixteen. After my marriage I had to work. I cut grass for fuel, carried firewood, and farmed. The housework and cooking were done by my mother-in-law, who also helped me in the fields. After she died, I took over all the responsibilities myself. No men helped me with the farm work, and we did not have the money to hire labourers. I did the plowing myself, even with a baby on my back. I cut grass and sold the grass and vegetables. I worked and struggled hard. I also worked for the Texaco company carrying steel and kerosene. In the evenings I wove patterned bands. I could weave one in two or three nights, but I never had time during the day (84-5).

"In their [Hakka] domestic life you find that there is not such a strict separation of the sexes as elsewhere. It strikes one favorably to see the whole family working together on the fields or to see men and women going together to the market town from the different villages to offer the produce of the soil for sale, and to purchase what they want." (Lechler 358) Marriage, the base of a family, was arranged by both sets of parents through a matchmaker. The Hakka usually practiced ethnic endogamy. They contracted for brides within the system of Hakka villages looking for an individual with a different surname (Berkowitz 14, Pasternak 62). The marriage was typically monogamous partially because poverty made polygamy unreasonable (Lechler 359). This is true for most poor peasants; it is not unique to the Hakka culture. Two types of marriages were practiced – minor marriage, where girls were sent at a young age to their intended husband's family, and major marriage where the girl, upon the wedding day, was transferred to her husband's family. Although women left their natal families upon marriage, their relationship with the "outside family" (their biological family) remained an important one. Young women went back for brief visits, with the permission of their mother's-in-law, especially at the New Year and for weddings and funerals (Johnson 1988; 143, 188).

The Hakka had no predisposition for major marriage (Pasternak 1983, 56). In fact, Dr. Charles Eitel noted, in 1841, that the frequency of minor marriage among the Hakka of the New Territories correlated to the relative infrequency of servant-slave girls, which were "comparatively rare among the Hakkas" while early betrothals and early marriages were especially common among the Hakka. The betrothed as soon as she was able to walk around, three or four years old, was sent to her future husband's family and remained there until her marriage. In that time she held exactly the same position and performed the same duties as a purchased servant girl (Pasternak 1983, 55-6). There may have been a tendency for a certain form of marriage

but this was not a cultural marker.

Cuisine

Women, directly involved in child care and agriculture, probably also were the main preparers of food. Stauffer reports that Hakka food is "on the average inferior in quality to that of the *Punti*, but better than most parts of North China." (352) Rice was used as the base of Hakka cooking with sweet potatoes mixed in to stretch the food. Wolfram Eberhard found a tale concerning the high importance of food and value of not wasting food. This was among the few Stage I references to food or its preparation (77). Food and its preparation therefore did not play an important role in defining the cultural identity of the Hakka.

In Stage II works food preparation took on a cultural identity. <u>The Cambridge Encyclopedia of</u>

China[12] characterized Hakka food as "almost an unclassifiable cuisine, which can be loosely included in the south but is really not much like any other Chinese style" and continued by saying it was distinctive and simple mountain cuisine, using fowl and pork with less oil and aquatic products then other Southern Chinese cooking. This, however, was contradicted by other authors who said that Hakka cooking as a rule was oilier and saltier then Cantonese food. An article in <u>Free China Review</u> (1993) goes beyond this saying Hakka cooking represents Hakka culture (Chang 25).

Winnie Chang, in an article, analyzed Hakka cooking in relationship to cultural identity. According to Chang, Hakka dishes were usually made with simple, less-expensive ingredients and prepared generally by steaming or stir-frying, which made food preparation

---

[12] Hook, Brian editor. <u>The Cambridge Encyclopedia of China</u>. Cons. Ed. Denis Twitchett. New edition. Cambridge: Cambridge University Press, 1991. 375.

quicker. Chang believed this was because the Hakka were hardworking, thrifty, and intelligent (25). Chang's analysis used generalized characteristics as a useful means to extol a positive Hakka cultural identity. Chang continued by pointing out that Hakka cooking reflected the group's history. The Hakka dishes integrated many cooking styles and ingredients found in the various provinces they had settled in during their migrations. This is clearly demonstrated by the use of rice, from South China, in their cooking.

According to Chang the Hakka believed salt and fat helped stimulate the appetite for more rice. The consumption of more rice provided extra energy for working long hours on the less productive lands that the Hakka possessed. As well, salt needed to be replenished because of perspiring in the long hours of work. Salt was also used to preserve foods. The Hakka historically lived in isolated areas where fresh meat was hard to obtain and needed to be preserved to stretch protein consumption throughout the year. The meat supplemented the vegetables that the Hakka grew in gardens that were also preserved for later consumption. With their frugal and utilitarian ways they used all parts of the animal carcasses and the vegetables. Food also held significance in the form of a gift to reward a kindness (26). Chang has woven together myth and daily utility to reinforce and extol Hakka cultural identity. Food preparation showed adaptation and indicated utility to the daily circumstances of the Hakka with some dishes that were distinctive to the Hakka culture but, generally, it cannot be used to define the Hakka cultural identity.

Architecture

Stage I writers made only a few comments on Hakka architecture. R. Lechler reported that:

> They [Hakka] live in poor houses, mostly built from unburned brick which are not always even plastered, and are protected from the wet by the far protruding roof, or by straw which is fixed on to the walls; but when such unburned brick walls come under the influence of the heavy rains, by leakage of the roof, they soon melt, and make the houses unsafe to live in. (As well Lechler noted that) I [Lechler] have seen three storied [Hakka] houses built of stone from the foundation to the roof, and besides walled in by a substantial adobe wall, to protect the inmates and their property. (359).

In the early twentieth century Hakka houses were reported to be white, clean and well constructed in rows (Hsieh 221, Stauffer 351). For the most part the Hakka occupied scattered, small agnatic villages and hamlets in the mountainous districts where the people, as George Campbell noted, are well housed (Broomhall 44;

Huntington 168; Pasternak 1983, 56). The few large cities the Hakka occupied were surrounded with substantial walls for protection (Wiens 6). This indicated that Hakka, like other cultural groups, lived in a range of dwellings of different construction and quality. What they did have, however, were some forms that were distinctive in architectural design. The three types, 1) rectangle 2) modified-rectangle and 3) circular are analyzed by Stage II authors.

All three types are multi-storied (which is rare in China except in crowded cities) with not only individual flats but also with more public rooms than blocks of flats usually have. This design emphasized communal solidarity and defense (Naquin & Rawski 78, Institute 59). The dwellings included living quarters, ancestral halls, communal guest halls, pens for livestock and grain storage facilities. It was like a village built together in one building (Boyd 103, Naquin & Rawski 175). Many of these dwellings can still be viewed today and are

presently in use.

Figure 8 -- Rectangular Hakka Houses

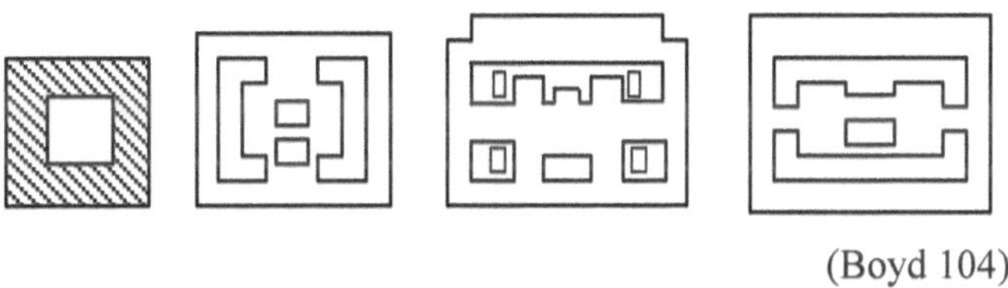

(Boyd 104)

The rectangular Hakka house (Figure 8) is a multi-storied structure. The north half typically has four stories and the south half has three. Access is provided to the stories by four staircases, one at each corner of the structure. There is a gallery on each floor that provides access to all the apartments. An Ancestral Hall is at the center of the north side on each floor. The kitchens are grouped on the ground floor along the outer walls of three sides of the structure. The last side, the south side, has the entrance and storage rooms (Boyd 103).

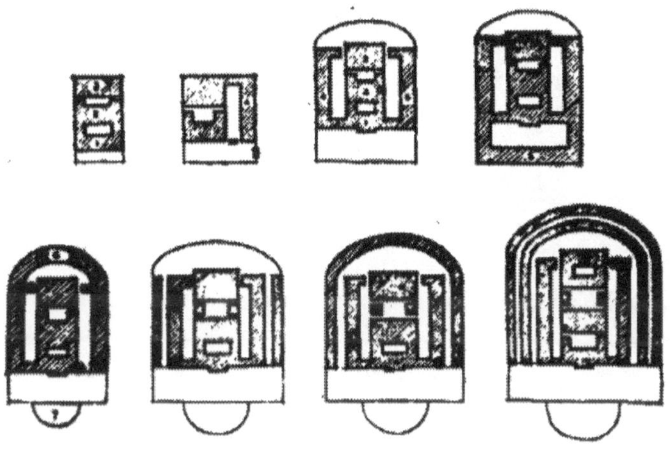

(Boyd 104)

The modified rectangle building style also is a multi-storied dwelling. (Figure 9) The north side has four stories while the east and west have either two or three stories. The central hall has one story and the south side has an open courtyard and often a semi-circular fish-pond. The entrances are on the east and west sides. The structure is divided into individual dwellings each with a kitchen. Staircases lead to each floor providing access to independent blocks with no balconies running along the floors. The ground floor

has groups of storage rooms and privies along the east

side (Boyd 105).

Figure 10 -- Circular Types of Hakka Houses

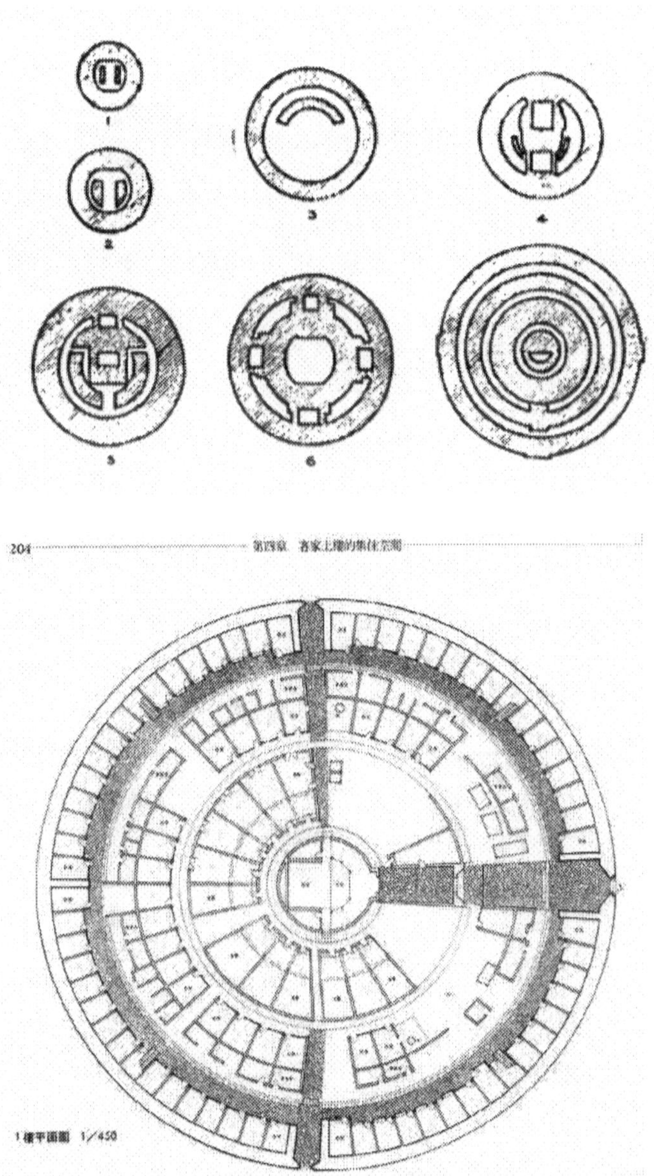

www.Chinadwelling.dk (also Boyd 105)

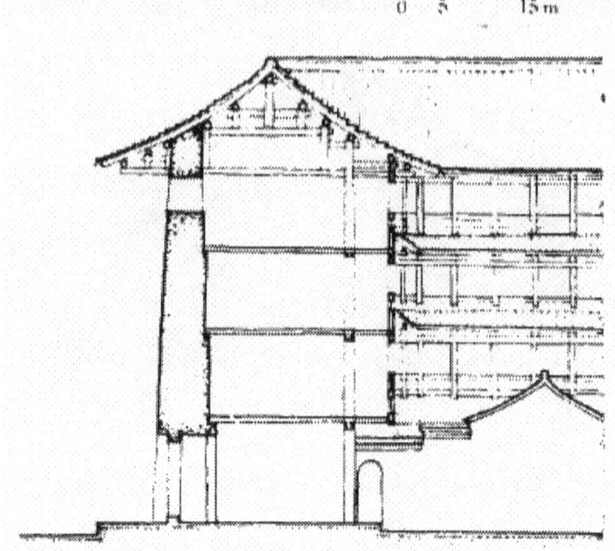

Schematic diagram of side view of Circular House

Figure 10
Circular House Interior Views[13]

---

[13] Circular House pictures from www.Asiawind.com

The circular architectural design was the most unusual for China. (Figure 10) The circular houses averaged in size from 20-30m (the largest known was 64m) and were composed of a group of three rings. The walls were made of rammed earth with bamboo strips inserted to add strength and wooden framework. Partition walls divided the interior space into rooms for different uses. The outermost ring was four stories with an average height of 13m and a thickness of 1.8m. Windows were only in the southern exterior wall on the third and fourth floors. This design facilitated defense of the community. The middle ring was two stories and the inner most ring was one story high.

The main entrances were on the southern and eastern exposure and large structures had minor entrances on the western and northern sides. Private dwellings or flats were accessible by balconies on each floor. Each floor also had a principle hall or room on the east side. The ground floor had groups of kitchens and stables for the cattle. The central courtyard provided access to staircases, a well, a mill, storage rooms, sheds for pigs and chickens and privies. As the other designs the individual dwellings and communal use areas opened into the center of the structure. This reinforced community solidarity and made the dwelling very defensible (Boyd 105, Institute 59).

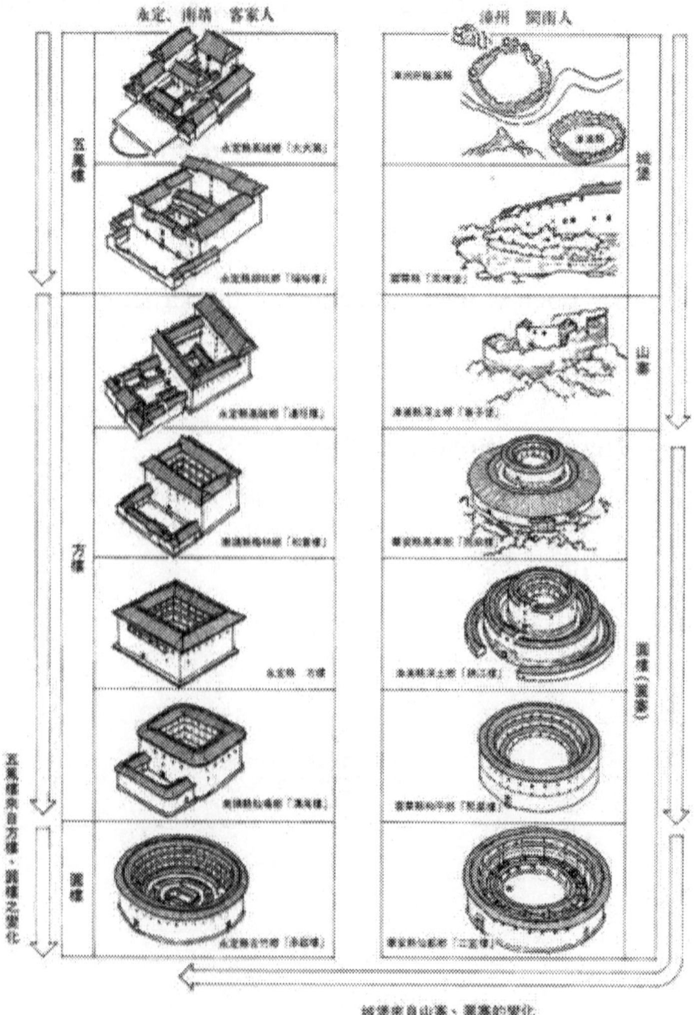

Figure 11 -- Hakka House Types

Worship

This solidarity also was found in their religious life. Hakka were considered intruders who could not share in the worship of local idols. Therefore, "they satisfy themselves with worshipping their ancestors" within their community (Piton 219) as Eberhard indicated "They cultivate a strong in-group feeling" (2). In preparation for a migration each family went to its fields or burial grounds to disinter the forefathers. The bones were carefully cleaned without water and placed in a clay jar called a golden urn. These jars were carried upon the men's backs for resettlement (Hsieh 159n). Upon reaching a new home a spot for a new grave was picked and the ancestors were reburied. If the bones could not be found or the family left in a hurry, a piece of clothing or other possession was taken and buried in a grave called a "clothes grave." If these items were lacking, a small silver or wooden tablet inscribed with the name and dates of birth and death was made. At the new grave site the spirit was called by name and enticed with food and tea to enter the tablet. After the spirit took possession of the tablet it was put into the prepared grave (Han 25-6). This movement of ancestors over great geographic distances set them apart from other Chinese cultures, who if they disinterred ancestors' bones for movement to a new burial site, always kept them within the same general geographic area.

Charles Piton said "they [Hakka] don't have proper ancestor's halls." Instead, they write the ancestors name on a paper and burn it while also burning incense and conducting ceremonies. The ashes were then put into a little bag and hung in the hall or some other part of the house (219). R. Lechler mentioned the "Hakkas are devoted to the three religions" but the Confucian precept of worshipping the dead is certainly the most cherished part of their religion.   Ancestral worship in the houses, in the ancestral halls, and on the hills where the tombs are, formed the most important part of their religious duties. With this they also performed blended Buddhist ceremonies on the occasion of deaths or funerals. "*Nan-wu-o-mi-t'o-fuh* is the Buddhist password that Hakkas use to pave the way to Happiness" and the Buddhistic *Kwan-yin's (Kon-yim-nyong)* name is written on big sheets of red paper above all other gods (357).

Herold J. Wiens wrote that "superstition is prevalent among the Hakka" (117). They believed that abnormal events foretold coming catastrophes and calamities while sorcerers (mediums) called *Shang-kung* or *Shang-p'o* (both males) performed spirit rapping so spirits could communicate by writing revelations about the future. The sorcerers also presided over ceremonies to drive out evil influences or cast out devils. The *Sien-*

poh was a sorcerer (shaman) that Lechler believed was a specific Hakka notion who was a conjurer of the dead. It was his place to inquire after the condition of the dead in Hades (Lechler 357).[14] Other gods worshipped by the Hakka, like *Wu Ti*, the god of war, mentioned in the Stage I writings are not unusual in Chinese cultures.

The missionaries hoped that the Hakka would leave these beliefs and become Christians. Many missions between 1846 and 1877 were set up in Hakka areas by the Germans, Americans and English (MacGillray 181). Lechler said in 1878 that the "Hakkas are not as bigoted as the Puntis, and the Gospel has found easier access to them than to the latter" (358). The missionaries also characterized the Hakka as a cultural group with "cleaner habits" they are "almost the only real Chinese who take daily baths" (Couling 222, Huntington 168). F. J. Wiens when he lived among the

---

[14] This is perhaps more a Christian notion than a Hakka concept.

Hakka observed that "Hakkas are a clean set of people. The bath in summer, with hot water, is a very important factor in their daily routine. As a whole, one may say of the Hakkas that they are as clean as one may expect in China" (7). Cleanliness may have been a convenient characteristic for the missionaries who had to send regular reports back to the home churches to ensure proper funding.

In their endeavor to convert the Hakka, the missionaries translated Christian ideology into the Hakka language. In 1847 Reverend Hamberg of the Basel Mission began a Hakka dictionary. Reverend Piton, also of the Basel Mission, reconstructed the Hakka dialect into characters by 1885. This assisted the work on the dictionary that went through many transitions before it was completed in 1905 by Reverend J. McIver of the English Presbyterian Mission. It contained 1,200 odd pages with phrases from Hakka dialect and a syllabary of the Hakka pronunciation of Chinese character in alphabetical order (Missionary News 1916, Stauffer 351). A. Nagel translated the *New Testament* into Hakka characters and O. Schultze did the *Old Testament* so that by 1916 a complete <u>Bible</u> was available in Hakka characters. Also, translations of the smaller and greater catechisms, a history of the <u>Bible</u>, a liturgy, a collection of sermons, children's hymns, a church paper and more were available in Hakka (Stauffer 351).

The missionaries met with success at the end of the nineteenth century when thousands of Hakka converted to Christianity. The Basel Mission especially became identified with the Hakka. Chart 4 shows the growth of the Basel Mission in Hakka regions. Missions provided western style education and employment that enabled Chinese Christians to attain positions as middlemen in both business and government.   This

afforded the Hakka upward mobility.

Chart 4 – Mission Schools

Basel Mission Schools and Churches
In the Hakka Regions of Guangdong

	Year	1876	1913	1948
Mission Stations		4	18	
Outstations		16	108	
Schools				
	theological seminary		1	
	normal		2	
	middle		1	
	secondary		4	
	boarding		13	
Students			3,097	
Communicants		953	6,699	20,000
Hospitals			2	
Dispensaries			Several	
European Staff			72	
Chinese Staff			271	

Conversion to Christianity meant change "in

name" at least. Christian Hakkas no longer worshipped

their ancestors in public – they many have continued this

practice in secret away from the Christian pastor's eyes -
- while in public they commemorated ancestors and
emphasized lineage. They did not worship idols but the
one "true God." For the *Punti*, who were suspicious of
the Christians and the Hakkas, these conversions to
Christianity fueled their hostility and the assertion that
Hakka would never have accepted the faith of the
foreign devils had they been "real" Chinese. To the
Punti the Hakka's acceptance of Christianity was
tantamount to abandoning Chinese identity (Constable
4).

Feuding Cultures

The high rate of conversion to Christianity was an indication of the Hakka rebellious spirit. As several Stage I writers indicated the Hakka were "turbulent and lawless people, and revolutionary and other secret societies flourished among them" (Broomhall 44). Ball and Richards concurred when they wrote that the Hakka were very contentious and were constantly engaged in lawsuits (Ball 280, Richards 343). This characteristic was attributed to the fact that the Hakka had migrated and lived in the mountains. Huntington said mountaineers all over the world were characterized by the love of liberty and the Hakka shared this nature (168).

The Hakka traditionally had been pushed to the poorer farm lands in *Guangdong*, often paying rent to the *Puntis*. The Hakka occupied a "marginal position wherever they lived" (Naquin 169). Their land was not able to support the growing population so they pushed into new areas. This brought them into closer contact with the *Punti* and conflict followed. The Hakka wanted *Punti* claimed land. Oftentimes, the land had little value and was so poor and rocky that it lay unused as the "*Punti* scorned to develop it." The Hakka also tried to purchase productive farms. Little by little moving from mountain homes displacing the natives the Hakka became feared and reviled (Huntington 167). The *Punti* tried to stop further Hakka immigration "by blocking attempts of recent Hakka immigrants to register with the local government" (Lo 95). This effectively blocked the Hakka from taking the local civil service examinations and from acquiring land.

These added animosities between the two groups led to clashes that lasted for over ten years (1854-1867) with casualties on both sides running into the hundreds of thousands.   Fighting broke out between villages "Puntis villages fought under the red flag and Hakkas under the white flag" (Lo 101).   Raiding parties were organized by both sides. At the start the Hakkas seemed to have the advantage but quickly their villages began to fall and Hakka families fled if they could.

The government had been busy with the British and French at this time and did not get involved in the local Hakka-*Punti* conflicts – so the fighting continued on and off for ten years.   The fighting was finally brought to a halt in 1867 when the governor of *Kwangtung, Chian I-li* decided to take charge. He made up his mind that the Hakkas were "bandits who probably harbored rebellious or treasonable intentions" (Lo 104). He sent his forces against them until they agreed to settlement terms.   To bring order many Hakka were resettled outside of the area.   In this instance the stereotype of the Hakka probably worked against them but it was a stereotype and not a cultural marker.

Another struggle, the *Taiping* Rebellion (1850-1864)[15] had similar origins. *Hung Hsiu-ch'uan,* a Hakka, had been inspired by Christian missionary tracts and was convinced that the alien *Manchus* were devils who must die if China were to live. He with his cousin *Feng Yunshan* formed the God Worshipping Society in 1850. Together they converted dozens of communities to their mission. For the most part the membership of the society was drawn from Hakka villages. Many had become discontent with poverty and the lack of options for land ownership.

The society established a base in the Thistle Mountain in *Guangxi*. In the next few years *Hong's* armies drew large numbers of people including non-

---

[15] There is an abundance of well written material on the Taiping Rebellion. The reader is encouraged to pursue additional readings to understand the full impact of this movement.

92

Hakka. He led his group to *Nanjing* – gaining control of a large area of Southern China. The armed conflict with the government, however, brought about the eventual downfall of the Heavenly Kingdom.

When Hong organized his armies he, with his officers, many of whom were also Hakka, incorporated certain attributes that can be traced to Hakka culture. Shih has said that "their [Hakka] sense of solidarity and willingness to die for one another in time of need gave substance to the idea of the brotherhood of men." He claims also, that "another contribution of the Hakkas was a sense of ethnic solidarity, which plays a great part in the Taiping ideology" (Shih 312).

The role of women in the Heavenly Kingdom was strikingly similar to the characteristics of women in the Hakka culture. Women were employed in much of the heavy labor of the camps, cooking, collecting firewood, making ropes etc. As well, they were formed into regiments of fighting units. Some were given roles of leadership over the women's quarters and over the female regiments. Selling girls into slavery, prostitution and foot binding were prohibited – clearly ideas that came from Hakka culture.

Cultural Markers Conclusion

Through the writings in the late nineteenth century and into the twentieth century a small piece of the cultural identity for the Hakka can be pieced together. What have been the characteristics associated with the Hakka? and Which are actual cultural markers? Chart 5 lists the characteristics that emerged in the works.

Chart 5 – Cultural Markers

Characteristic	Stereotype	Cultural Marker
Architecture		Some forms
Chinese Origin		Not definite
Cleanliness	X	
Diligent	X	
Distinctive Female Dress		Culturally distinctive
Distinctive Language		X
Distinctive Food		Some dishes
History of Migration		X
Honest	X	
Intelligent	X	
Patriotic	X	
Religion	X	
Singing		Culturally distinctive
Value Education	X	
Women do hard labor		Gender role difference
Women -- unbound feet		Culturally distinctive

Chart 5 illustrates that most characteristics which have been associated with the Hakka are actually stereotypes. They have been applied to convey either a positive or negative image. Women's job roles, unbound feet and clothing can be culturally distinctive but not really cultural marker. Some of the architecture can be a cultural marker but not all forms. Courting and love songs are found among some of the minority groups, but not among proper Han subgroups. The only clear cultural markers that distinguish the Hakka from Han Chinese are language and a history of migration.

BIBLIOGRAPHY I

STAGE I

<u>**Group One**</u>

1854   Hamberg, Theodore. <u>The Visions of Hung-Siu-Tshuen, and Origin of the Kwang-si Insurrection</u>. Hong Kong: China Mail Office, 1854.

1867   "The Hakka War." <u>North China Herald and Market Report</u>. 29 June 1867: 133.

1867   Eitel, E. J. "Ethnographical Sketches of the Hakka Chinese," <u>The China Review: or Notes and Queries on the Far East</u>. 1867. 20 (1894-1895): 263-7.

1870   Piton, Charles. "The Hia-K'ah in the Chekiang Province, and the Hakka in the Canton Province," <u>Chinese Recorder and Missionary Journal</u>. (Jan. 1870): 218-220.

1878   Lechler, R[udolph]. "The Hakka Chinese." <u>Chinese Recorder and Missionary Journal</u>. Sept. – Oct. 1878: 352-359.

1891   "Missionary News." <u>Chinese Recorder and Missionary Journal</u>. May 1891: 240.

1897 Johnston, Ja[mes]s. <u>China and Formosa: The Story of the Mission of the Presbyterian Church of England</u>. 1897. Taipei: Ch'eng Wen Publishing Company, 1972.

1909 Ebert, W. "Mission Work Amongst the Chinese of British North Borneo." <u>Chinese Recorder and Missionary Journal</u>. Sept. 1909: 487.

1910 Mission, E. P. "In Memoriam – Rev. D. MacIver." <u>Chinese Recorder and Missionary Journal</u>. Aug. 1910. 548-553.

1912 Campbell, George. "Origin and Migrations of the Hakkas." <u>Chinese Recorder and Missionary Journal.</u> Aug. 1912: 473-480.

1916 Schultze, Otto. "The Policy of the Basel Mission Among the Hakkas," <u>Chinese Recorder and Missionary Journal</u>. Nov. 1916. 743-758.

1918 MacKenzie, M. C. "Biographical Sketch of Rev. Phang Vun-san of Wukingfu College," <u>Chinese Recorder and Missionary Journal</u>. March 1918. 181-186.

192? Wiens, F. J. <u>Fifteen Years Among the Hakkas of South China</u>. N.p.: n.p., n.d. [192?].

<u>Group Two</u>

1883 Williams, Samual Wells. <u>The Middle Kingdom: A Survey of the Geography, Government, Literature, Social Life, Arts, and History</u>. Vol. II. New York: Charles Scribner's Sons, 1883.

1886   Henry Benjamin Couch. Ling-Nam or Interior Views of Southern China: Including Explorations in the Hitherto Untraversed Island of Hainan. London: S. W. Partridge and Co., 1886.

1905   Little, Archibald. The Far East. Oxford: Clarendon Press, 1905.

1907   Broomhall, Marshall, ed. The Chinese Empire: A General & Missionary Survey. London: Morgan & Scott, 1907.

1907   MacGillivray D. Editor. A Century of Protestant Missions in China (1807 – 1907): Being The Centenary Conference Historical Volume. 1907. San Francisco: Chinese Materials Center, Inc., 1979.

1908   Richards, L. Comprehensive Geography of the Chinese Empire and Dependencies. Trans. M. Kennelly. Shanghai: T'usewei Press, 1908.

1917   Couling, Samuel. The Encyclopaedia Sinica. London: Oxford University Press, Humphrey Milford, 1917.

1922   Stauffer, Milton T., ed. The Christian Occupation of China: A General Survey of the Numerical Strength and Geographical Distruibuton [sic] of the Christian Forces in China Made by the Special Committee on Survey and Occupation China Continuation Committee 1918-1921. Shanghai: China Continuation Committee, 1922.

1925   Ball, J. Dyer. Things Chinese; or, Notes
       Connected With China. Fifth Edition, Revised
       by E. Chalmers Werner. Shanghai: Kelly &
       Walsh, Limited, 1925.

1927   Huntington, Ellsworth. The Character of Races:
       As Influenced by Physical Environment, Natural
       Selection and Historical Development. New
       York: Charles Scribner's Sons, 1927.

1928   Li, Chi. The Formation of the Chinese People:
       An Anthropological Inquiry. Cambridge:
       Harvard University Press, 1928.

1929   Hsieh T'ing-Yu. "Origin and Migrations of the
       Hakkas." The Chinese Social and Political
       Science Review. 13, 2 (April 1929): 202-226.

1948   Forrest, R[obert] A. D. The Chinese Language.
       1948. London: Faber and Faber Ltd., 1973.

1954   Wiens, Herold J. Han Chinese Expansion in
       South China. Org. pub. as China's March
       Toward the Tropics. 1954. [US] N.p.: The Shoe
       String Press, Inc., 1967.

1965   Han Suyin. The Crippled Tree: China
       Biography, History Autobiography. New York:
       G. P. Putnam's Sons, 1965.[16]

1974   Eberhard, Wolfram. Studies in Hakka Folktales.
       Taiwan: The Orient Cultural Service, 1974.[17]

---

[16] The information used from this book was primarily based on
stories told to the author, therefore, the book has been categorized
as a Stage I book.

Stage II

1960   Pratt, Jean A. "Emigration and Unilineal Descent Groups: A Study of Marriage in a Hakka Village in the New Territories, Hong Kong," The Eastern Antropologist. 13, 4 (June – Aug. 1960): 147-158.

1962   Boyd, Andrew. Chinese Architecture and Town Planning: 1500 B.C. – A.D. 1911. Chicago: The University of Chicago Press, 1962.

1965   Wan Lo. "Communal Strife in Mid-Nineteenth-Century Kwangtung: The Establishment of Ch'ih-ch'i," Papers on China. 19 (Dec. 1965): 85-119.

1966   Wakeman, Frederic Jr. Strangers at the Gate: Social Disorder in South China, 1839-1861. Berkeley: University of California Press, 1966.

1967   Aijmer, Göran. "Expansion and Extension in Hakka Society," Journal of the Hong Kong Branch of the Royal Asiatic Society. 7 (1967): 42-79.

1967   Fallers, L. A. Immigrants and Associations. The Hague: Mouton, 1967.

1967   Shih, Vincent Y. C. The Taiping Ideology: Its Sources, Interpretations, and Influences. Seattle: University of Washington Press, 1967.

---

[17] Ibid.

1968 Cohen, Myron L. "The Hakka or 'Guest People': Dialect as a Sociocultural Variable in Southeastern China." <u>Ethnohistory</u>. 15, 3 (Summer, 1968): 237-292.

1968 Ping-ti Ho and Tang Tsou, eds. <u>China's Heritage and the Communist Political System</u>. Book Two. Chicago: The University of Chicago Press, 1968.

1969 Berkowitz, Morris I., Frederick P. Brandauer, and John H. Reed. <u>Folk Religion in an Urban Setting: A Study of Hakka Villagers in Transition</u>. Hong Kong: the Christian Study Centre on Chinese Religion and Culture, 1969.

1969 Char, Tin-Yuke & C. H. Kwock. <u>The Hakka Chinese: Their Origin & Folk Songs</u>. San Francisco: Jade Mountain Press, 1969.

1972 Pasternak, Burton. <u>Kinship & Community in Two Chinese Villages</u>. Stanford: Stanford University Press, 1972.

1973 Alley, Rewi. <u>Travels in China: 1966-71</u>. Peking: New World Press, 1973.

1975 Nakagawa, Manabu. "Studies on the History of the Hakkas: Reconsidered," <u>The Developing Economies</u>. 13, 2 (June 1975): 208-223.

1975 Wakeman, Frederic Jr. <u>The Fall of Imperial China</u>. New York: The Free Press, 1975.

1976   Cohen, Myron L. <u>House United, House Divided: The Chinese Family in Taiwan</u>. New York: Columbia University Press, 1976.

1976   Johnson, Elizabeth L. "'Patterned Bands' in the New Territories of Hong Kong." <u>Journal of the Hong Kong Branch of the Royal Asiatic Society</u>. 16 (1976): 81-91.

1977   Alley, Rewi. "Meihsien: The Great Hakka Centre," <u>Eastern Horizon</u>. 16, 5 (May 1977): 16-30.

1977   Curwen, C. A. <u>Taiping Rebel: The Deposition of Li Hsiu-Ch'eng</u>. Cambridge: Cambridge University Press, 1977.

1977   Kuhn, Philip A. "Origins of the Taiping Vision: Cross-Cultural Dimensions of a Chinese Rebellion," <u>Comparative Studies in Society and History</u>. 19, 3 (July 1977): 350-366.

1978   Kazuko, Ono. <u>The Chinese Women in a Century of Revolution: 1850-1950</u>. 1978. Trans. Kathryn Bernhardt, Timothy Brook, Joshua A. Fogel, Jonathan Lipman, Susan Mann and Laurel Rhodes. Edited by Joshua A. Fogel. Stanford: Stanford University Press, 1989.

1980   Kuhn, Philip A. <u>Rebellion and Its Enemies in Late Imperial China: Militarization and Social Structure, 1796-1864</u>. 1970. Cambridge: Harvard University Press, 1980.

1981   Blake, C. Fred. <u>Ethnic Groups and Social Change in a Chinese Market Town</u>. Asian

Studies at Hawaii 27. Hawaii: The University
Press of Hawaii, 1981.

1981   Lamley, Harry J. "Subethnic Rivalry in the
Ch'ing Period," In The Anthropology of
Taiwanese Society. Edited by Emily Martin
Ahern and Hill Gates. Stanford: Stanford
University Press, 1981.

1983   Averill, Stephen C. "The Shed People and the
Opening of the Yangzi Highlands," Modern
China. 9, 1: (Jan. 1983): 84-126.

1983   Pasternak, Burton. Guests in the Dragon: Social
Demography of a Chinese District 1895-1946.
New York: Columbia University Press, 1983.

1985   Jiann Hsieh. "An Old Bottle with a New Brew:
The Waichow Hakkas' Associations in Hong
Kong." Human Organization. 44, 2 (Summer
1985): 154-161.

1985   Leong, S. T. "The Hakka Chinese of Lingnan:
Ethnicity and Social Change in Modern Times,"
in Ideal and Reality: Social and Political Change
in Modern China: 1860-1949. Edited by David
Pong and Edmund S. K. Fung. Lanham:
University Press of America, Inc., 1985.

1985   Moser, Leo J. The Chinese Mosaic: The
Peoples and Provinces of China. Boulder:
Westview Press, 1985.

1985   Smith, Earl T. Chinese Christians: Élites,
Middlemen, and the Church in Hong Kong.
Hong Kong: Oxford University Press, 1985.

1986   Chinese Academy of Architecture. <u>Classical Chinese Architecture</u>. 2nd ed. Trans. Wong Chi Kui & Chung Wah Nan. Hong Kong: Joint Publishing Co., 1986.

1986   Institute of the History of Natural Sciences Chinese Academy of Sciences. <u>History and Development of Ancient Chinese Architecture</u>. Beijing: Science Press, 1986.

1987   Naquin, Susan & Evelyn S. Rawski. <u>Chinese Society in the Eighteenth Century</u>. New Haven: Yale University Press, 1987.

1987   Ramsey, S. Robert. <u>The Languages of China</u>. Princeton: Princeton University Press, 1987.

1988   Johnson, Elizabeth L. "Grieving for the Dead, Grieving for the Living: Funeral Laments of Hakka Women," in <u>Death Ritual in Late Imperial and Modern China</u>. Edited by James L. Watson and Evelyn S. Rawski. Berkeley: University of California Press, 1988.

1988   Norman, Jerry. <u>Chinese</u>. Cambridge: Cambridge University Press, 1988.

1989   Herberer, Thomas. <u>China and Its National Minorities: Autonomy or Assimilation?</u>. Armonk: M.E. Sharpe, Inc., 1989.

1990   Spence, Jonathan D. <u>The Search For Modern China</u>. New York: W. W. Norton & Company, 1990.

1991   Kiang, Clyde. The Hakka Search for a
        Homeland. Elgin: Allegheny Press, 1991.

1991   Martin, Howard J. "Hakka Mausoleums in
        North Taiwan," Ethnology. 30, 1 (Jan. 1991):
        85-99.

1992   Constable, Nicole. The Village of Humble
        Worship: Religion and Ethnicity in a Hakka
        Protestant Community in Hong Kong. Diss.
        University of California, Berkeley, 1989. Ann
        Arbor: UMI, 1992. 9006290.

1992   Erbaugh, Mary S. "The Chinese Revolution as a
        Hakka Enterprise." The China Quarterly. (Dec.
        1992): 937-968.

1993   Chang, Winnie. "Home Cooking With a
        History." Free China Review. 43, 10 (Oct. 93):
        24-31.

1993   Yun, Eugenia. "The Invisible Group," Free
        China Review. 43, 10 (Oct. 93): 24-31.

1993   Free China Review. 43, 10 (Oct. 93): 4-39.
        Several Articles

BIBLIOGRAPHY II

Aijmer, Göran. "Expansion and Extension in Hakka Society," <u>Journal of the Hong Kong Branch of the Royal Asiatic Society</u>. 7 (1967): 42-79.

Alley, Rewi. "Meihsien: The Great Hakka Centre," <u>Eastern Horizon</u>. 16, 5 (May 1977): 16-30.

Alley, Rewi. <u>Travels in China: 1966-71</u>. Peking: New World Press, 1973.

Averill, Stephen C. "The Shed People and the Opening of the Yangzi Highlands," <u>Modern China</u>. 9, 1: (Jan. 1983): 84-126.

Ball, J. Dyer. <u>Things Chinese; or, Notes Connected With China</u>. Fifth Edition, Revised by E. Chalmers Werner. Shanghai: Kelly & Walsh, Limited, 1925.

Berkowitz, Morris I., Frederick P. Brandauer, and John H. Reed. <u>Folk Religion in an Urban Setting: A Study of Hakka Villagers in Transition</u>. Hong Kong: the Christian Study Centre on Chinese Religion and Culture, 1969.

Blake, C. Fred. <u>Ethnic Groups and Social Change in a Chinese Market Town</u>. Asian Studies at Hawaii

27. Hawaii: The University Press of Hawaii, 1981.

Boyd, Andrew. Chinese Architecture and Town Planning: 1500 B.C. – A.D. 1911. Chicago: The University of Chicago Press, 1962.

Broomhall, Marshall, ed. The Chinese Empire: A General & Missionary Survey. London: Morgan & Scott, 1907.

Campbell, George. "Origin and Migrations of the Hakkas." Chinese Recorder and Missionary Journal. Aug. 1912: 473-480.

Chang, Winnie. "Home Cooking With a History." Free China Review. 43, 10 (Oct. 93): 24-31.

Char, Tin-Yuke & C. H. Kwock. The Hakka Chinese: Their Origin & Folk Songs. San Francisco: Jade Mountain Press, 1969.

Chinese Academy of Architecture. Classical Chinese Architecture. 2nd ed. Trans. Wong Chi Kui & Chung Wah Nan. Hong Kong: Joint Publishing Co., 1986.

Cohen, Myron L. "The Hakka or 'Guest People': Dialect as a Sociocultural Variable in Southeastern China." Ethnohistory. 15, 3 (Summer, 1968): 237-292.

Cohen, Myron L. House United, House Divided: The Chinese Family in Taiwan. New York: Columbia University Press, 1976.

Constable, Nicole. <u>The Village of Humble Worship:
          Religion and Ethnicity in a Hakka Protestant
          Community in Hong Kong</u>. Diss. University of
          California, Berkeley, 1989. Ann Arbor: UMI,
          1992. 9006290.

Couling, Samuel. <u>The Encyclopaedia Sinica</u>. London:
          Oxford University Press, Humphrey Milford,
          1917.

Curwen, C. A. <u>Taiping Rebel: The Deposition of Li
          Hsiu-Ch'eng</u>. Cambridge: Cambridge
          University Press, 1977.

Eberhard, Wolfram. <u>Studies in Hakka Folktales</u>.
          Taiwan: The Orient Cultural Service, 1974.

Ebert, W. "Mission Work Amongst the Chinese of
          British North Borneo." <u>Chinese Recorder and
          Missionary Journal</u>. Sept. 1909: 487.

Eitel, E. J. "Ethnographical Sketches of the Hakka
          Chinese," <u>The China Review: or Notes and
          Queries on the Far East</u>. 1867. 20 (1894-1895):
          263-7.

Erbaugh, Mary S. "The Chinese Revolution as a Hakka
          Enterprise." <u>The China Quarterly</u>. (Dec. 1992):
          937-968.

Fallers, L. A. <u>Immigrants and Associations</u>. The
          Hague: Mouton, 1967.

Forrest, R[obert] A. D. <u>The Chinese Language</u>. 1948.
          London: Faber and Faber Ltd., 1973.

Free China Review. 43, 10 (Oct. 93): 4-39. *Several Articles*

"The Hakka War." North China Herald and Market Report. 29 June 1867: 133.

Hamberg, Theodore. The Visions of Hung-Siu-Tshuen, and Origin of the Kwang-si Insurrection. Hong Kong: China Mail Office, 1854.

Han Suyin. The Crippled Tree: China Biography, History Autobiography. New York: G. P. Putnam's Sons, 1965.

Henry Benjamin Couch. Ling-Nam or Interior Views of Southern China: Including Explorations in the Hitherto Untraversed Island of Hainan. London: S. W. Partridge and Co., 1886.

Herberer, Thomas. China and Its National Minorities: Autonomy or Assimilation?. Armonk: M.E. Sharpe, Inc., 1989.

Hsieh T'ing-Yu. "Origin and Migrations of the Hakkas." The Chinese Social and Political Science Review. 13, 2 (April 1929): 202-226.

Huntington, Ellsworth. The Character of Races: As Influenced by Physical Environment, Natural Selection and Historical Development. New York: Charles Scribner's Sons, 1927.

Institute of the History of Natural Sciences Chinese Academy of Sciences. History and Development of Ancient Chinese Architecture. Beijing: Science Press, 1986.

Jiann Hsieh. "An Old Bottle with a New Brew: The
     Waichow Hakkas' Associations in Hong Kong."
     Human Organization. 44, 2 (Summer 1985):
     154-161.

Johnson, Elizabeth L. "Grieving for the Dead, Grieving
     for the Living: Funeral Laments of Hakka
     Women," in Death Ritual in Late Imperial and
     Modern China. Edited by James L. Watson and
     Evelyn S. Rawski. Berkeley: University of
     California Press, 1988.

Johnston, Ja[mes]s. China and Formosa: The Story of
     the Mission of the Presbyterian Church of
     England. 1897. Taipei: Ch'eng Wen Publishing
     Company, 1972.

Kazuko, Ono. The Chinese Women in a Century of
     Revolution: 1850-1950. 1978. Trans. Kathryn
     Bernhardt, Timothy Brook, Joshua A. Fogel,
     Jonathan Lipman, Susan Mann and Laurel
     Rhodes. Edited by Joshua A. Fogel. Stanford:
     Stanford University Press, 1989.

Kiang, Clyde. The Hakka Search for a Homeland.
     Elgin: Allegheny Press, 1991.

Kuhn, Philip A. "Origins of the Taiping Vision: Cross-
     Cultural Dimensions of a Chinese Rebellion,"
     Comparative Studies in Society and History. 19,
     3 (July 1977): 350-366.

Kuhn, Philip A. Rebellion and Its Enemies in Late
     Imperial China: Militarization and Social
     Structure, 1796-1864. 1970. Cambridge:
     Harvard University Press, 1980.

Lamley, Harry J. "Subethnic Rivalry in the Ch'ing
        Period," In <u>The Anthropology of Taiwanese
        Society</u>. Edited by Emily Martin Ahern and Hill
        Gates. Stanford: Stanford University Press,
        1981.

Lechler, R[udolph]. "The Hakka Chinese." <u>Chinese
        Recorder and Missionary Journal</u>. Sept. – Oct.
        1878: 352-359.

Leong, S. T. "The Hakka Chinese of Lingnan:
        Ethnicity and Social Change in Modern Times,"
        in <u>Ideal and Reality: Social and Political Change
        in Modern China: 1860-1949</u>. Edited by David
        Pong and Edmund S. K. Fung. Lanham:
        University Press of America, Inc., 1985.

Li, Chi. <u>The Formation of the Chinese People: An
        Anthropological Inquiry</u>. Cambridge: Harvard
        University Press, 1928.

Little, Archibald. <u>The Far East</u>. Oxford: Clarendon
        Press, 1905.

MacGillivray D. Editor. <u>A Century of Protestant
        Missions in China (1807 – 1907): Being The
        Centenary Conference Historical Volume</u>. 1907.
        San Francisco: Chinese Materials Center, Inc.,
        1979.

MacKenzie, M. C. "Biographical Sketch of Rev. Phang
        Vun-san of Wukingfu College," <u>Chinese
        Recorder and Missionary Journal</u>. March 1918.
        181-186.

Martin, Howard J. "Hakka Mausoleums in North
        Taiwan," <u>Ethnology</u>. 30, 1 (Jan. 1991): 85-99.

"Missionary News." <u>Chinese Recorder and Missionary
        Journal</u>. May 1891: 240.

Mission, E. P. "In Memoriam – Rev. D. MacIver."
        <u>Chinese Recorder and Missionary Journal</u>. Aug.
        1910. 548-553.

Moser, Leo J. <u>The Chinese Mosaic: The Peoples and
        Provinces of China</u>. Boulder: Westview Press,
        1985.

Nakagawa, Manabu. "Studies on the History of the
        Hakkas: Reconsidered," <u>The Developing
        Economies</u>. 13, 2 (June 1975): 208-223.

Naquin, Susan & Evelyn S. Rawski. <u>Chinese Society in
        the Eighteenth Century</u>. New Haven: Yale
        University Press, 1987.

Norman, Jerry. <u>Chinese</u>. Cambridge: Cambridge
        University Press, 1988.

Pasternak, Burton. <u>Guests in the Dragon: Social
        Demography of a Chinese District 1895-1946</u>.
        New York: Columbia University Press, 1983.

Pasternak, Burton. <u>Kinship & Community in Two
        Chinese Villages</u>. Stanford: Stanford University
        Press, 1972.

Ping-ti Ho and Tang Tsou, eds. <u>China's Heritage and
        the Communist Political System</u>. Book Two.

Chicago: The University of Chicago Press, 1968.

Piton, Charles. "The Hia-K'ah in the Chekiang Province, and the Hakka in the Canton Province," <u>Chinese Recorder and Missionary Journal</u>. (Jan. 1870): 218-220.

Pratt, Jean A. "Emigration and Unilineal Descent Groups: A Study of Marriage in a Hakka Village in the New Territories, Hong Kong," <u>The Eastern Antropologist</u>. 13, 4 (June – Aug. 1960): 147-158.

Ramsey, S. Robert. <u>The Languages of China</u>. Princeton: Princeton University Press, 1987.

Richards, L. <u>Comprehensive Geography of the Chinese Empire and Dependencies</u>. Trans. M. Kennelly. Shanghai: T'usewei Press, 1908.

Schultze, Otto. "The Policy of the Basel Mission Among the Hakkas," <u>Chinese Recorder and Missionary Journal</u>. Nov. 1916. 743-758.

Shih, Vincent Y. C. <u>The Taiping Ideology: Its Sources, Interpretations, and Influences</u>. Seattle: University of Washington Press, 1967.

Smith, Earl T. <u>Chinese Christians: Élites, Middlemen, and the Church in Hong Kong</u>. Hong Kong: Oxford University Press, 1985.

Spence, Jonathan D. <u>The Search For Modern China</u>. New York: W. W. Norton & Company, 1990.

Stauffer, Milton T., ed. The Christian Occupation of
        China: A General Survey of the Numerical
        Strength and Geographical Distruibuton [sic] of
        the Christian Forces in China Made by the
        Special Committee on Survey and Occupation
        China Continuation Committee 1918-1921.
        Shanghai: China Continuation Committee,
        1922.

Wakeman, Frederic Jr. Strangers at the Gate: Social
        Disorder in South China, 1839-1861. Berkeley:
        University of California Press, 1966.

Wakeman, Frederic Jr. The Fall of Imperial China.
        New York: The Free Press, 1975.

Wan Lo. "Communal Strife in Mid-Nineteenth-Century
        Kwangtung: The Establishment of Ch'ih-ch'i,"
        Papers on China. 19 (Dec. 1965): 85-119.

Wiens, F. J. Fifteen Years Among the Hakkas of South
        China. N.p.: n.p., n.d. [192?].

Wiens, Herold J. Han Chinese Expansion in South
        China. Org. pub. as China's March Toward the
        Tropics. 1954. [US] N.p.: The Shoe String
        Press, Inc., 1967.

Williams, Samual Wells. The Middle Kingdom: A
        Survey of the Geography, Government,
        Literature, Social Life, Arts, and History. Vol.
        II. New York: Charles Scribner's Sons, 1883.

Yun, Eugenia. "The Invisible Group," Free China
        Review. 43, 10 (Oct. 93): 24-31.